Contents

Before We Begin.. 4

Introduction 10

How Investing Works... 12
   Your Portfolio... 34

Asset Management... 37

Guide to Asset Classes... 55
   What Are Equities?... 56
   What Are Bonds?.. 60
   What is Cash?... 64
   What is Property?.. 66
   What Are Commodities?.. 68

That's How Asset Management Works!............................ 70

Asset Management Words... 72

About the Project.. 76

Before We Begin...

How the World Really Works
ASSET MANAGEMENT

Published by Guy Fox History Project Limited
Illustrated by Students at Moreland Primary School, London

How the World Really Works: Asset Management

Guy Fox History Project Limited

FIRST EDITION

Copyright © 2018 Guy Fox History Project Limited and Guy Fox Limited

www.guyfox.org.uk

All rights reserved. No part of this publication may be reproduced, photocopied, stored in a retrieval system, or transmitted in any form or by any means, electronic, mechanical or otherwise, without the prior permission of Guy Fox History Project Limited.

This book was illustrated with assistance from students at Moreland Primary School, whose drawings are used with their kind permission.

Schroders

Funded by Schroders plc and supported by their employees

Printed and bound in the UK

Of course.

An asset is something that has value, which can be sold or used as money.

A few explanations to get you started:

To invest is when you put money into something in the hope that it will make more money.

An investor is the person or institution that makes an investment.

Capital is the money used to make an investment.

An investment (also called an 'asset') is the 'something' that you put your money into.

And a return is the 'more money' that you hope to get back!

At the end of this book, you'll find a glossary of Asset Management Words; it includes all the words marked in DARK RED in the book.

Introduction

The purpose of Asset Management is simple:

To help investors reach their investing goals.

To understand how they do this, you'll need to know a bit about investing and how different investments work.

That's why we created this book!

HOW INVESTING WORKS

Investing is a way that your money can make money.

Here's the process.

INVESTING

Put capital into an asset.

Give it time and, hopefully, it will go up in value.

Get a return that is larger than the amount you invested!

3 Investing is risky. You might invest your capital and get NOTHING in return!

"You mean I could lose ALL my capital?"

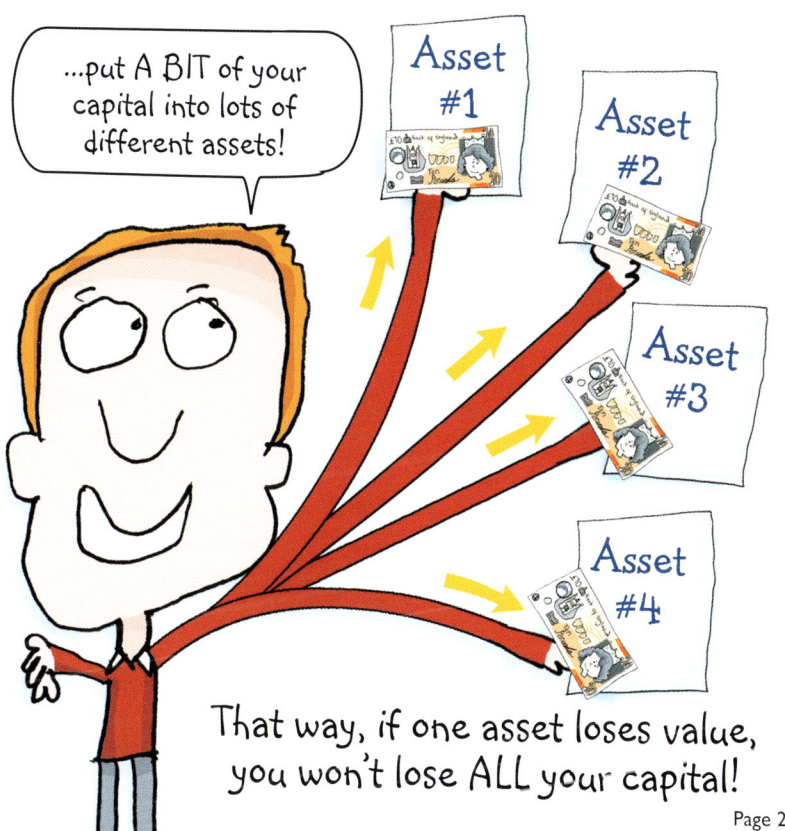

5 Investments are divided into asset classes:

Ownership of a Tiny Bit of a Big, Big Company

Equities

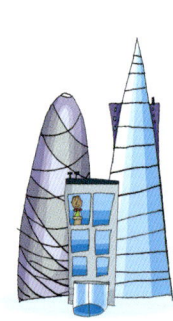

Property

'IOU' from a Big, Big Company or a Government Institution

Bonds

Cash

Commodities

6 There are special *financial markets* and *exchanges*, where assets are bought & sold.

Equities Market

Commodities Exchange

Bond Market

BONDS FOR SALE

In these markets, traders buy and sell assets for investors.

⑧ When you buy or sell your assets, you may have to pay a fee.

And you may also have to pay
capital gains tax on your returns!

9 The government makes regulations to control and oversee investing and to protect investors.

That's How Investing Works!

1. When you invest in something, you can't use that capital for anything else.
2. The value of assets can go up and down. You might lose some – or ALL – of your capital!
3. All investing has some level of risk.
4. You can diversify your capital in lots of ways.
5. There are different types of investments (called 'asset classes') and they work differently.
6. There are special financial markets, where traders buy and sell assets.
7. Assets require time and management.
8. When you buy & sell assets, you may have to pay fees and taxes.
9. The government supports investing by making regulations and overseeing investing activities.

Your Portfolio

Hold it! How can I manage ALL of that?!!
Eek!
How can I know the right time to divest to get the best return?
How can I diversify my capital into LOTS of assets and track the performance of them all?
How can I know which assets are high risk and which ones are low risk?
How can I get a good return on my capital?
How can I decide where to invest next?
How can I reach my goal?

In fact, Asset Management firms can help LOTS of investors reach their goals.

To help them, an Asset Management firm offers investors the chance to invest in a fund.

Each fund is created with a goal in mind.

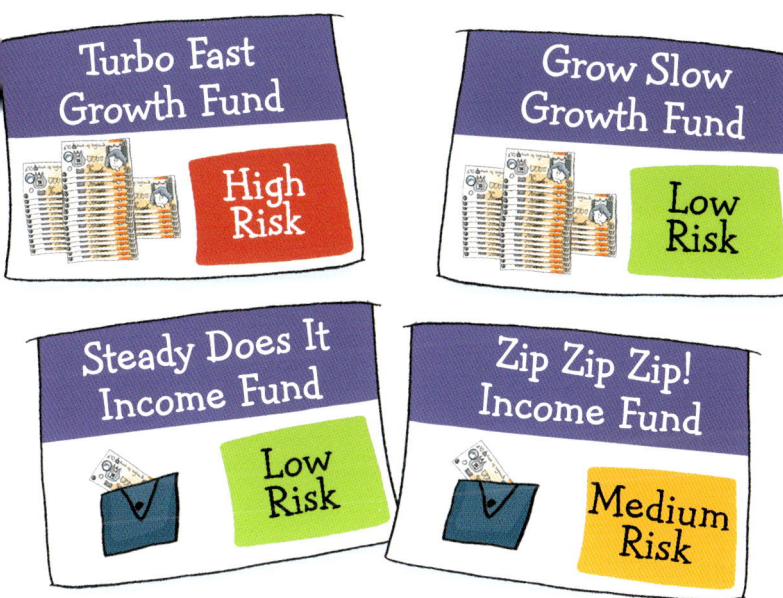

Here's How Fund Investing Works:
Lots of investors put capital into a fund.

The team searches for assets that are undervalued, which it thinks are likely to give good returns.

If those assets go UP in value and give positive returns, then the value of the fund will go UP.

Big Digger Company

A fund management team has experts who actively manage the fund.

The Asset Management firm charges investors fees for managing the fund.

If the Fund Management team makes good decisions, investors can achieve their goals!

So that's Asset Management!

Asset Management firms pool the capital of LOTS of investors and create funds.

Each fund has a different goal.

They diversify each fund into different assets.

They manage the fund — buying & selling assets at the right time — to get the best return for investors.

By investing in a fund, rather than directly, investors can invest in asset classes that would be too expensive for them.

Plus, investors get the benefit of diversification and the expertise of the Asset Managers.

Guide to Asset Classes

"If you're curious about asset classes, you've come to the right place!"

ASSET CLASSES

- Equities
- Bonds
- Cash
- Property
- Commodities

What Are Equities?

When a big, big company needs capital, it can sell part of itself by issuing *equities*.

How Equities Investing Works:

When you invest in equities, you're buying a tiny share of a big, big company. You buy the share at its current market value.

If the big, big company does well, the value of its shares will go up. Yippee!

But if the big, big company doesn't do well, the value of its shares will go down. Boo!

You can sell your shares, hopefully for more than you paid. That's your return!

You might also receive a dividend, which is a tiny bit of the company's profit.

Equity investing can be HIGH RISK or LOW RISK — or anywhere in between!

Those factors affect demand: How many investors want to own a tiny bit of that company?

If lots of investors want to own this company's shares, the value will go up.

If nobody wants to own that company's shares, the value will go down.

What Are Bonds?

If a government or big, big company needs capital, it may not be able to get a loan from a bank.

"We need capital to expand the airport, so we're issuing a bond."

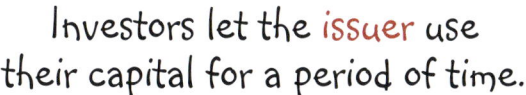

Here's an example:

How Bond Investing Works:

When you invest in a bond, you're letting a government or big, big company use your capital for a period of time. This is called the 'term'.

Throughout this term, the issuer pays you regular interest. That's your return!

Plus, at the end of the term the bond reaches maturity and you'll get your capital back.

There is a risk that the issuer might default and NOT give you back your capital!

Investing in bonds is usually LOW RISK and usually offers low returns.
(Of course, it all depends on the type of bond and what's happening in the bond market!)

This asset class is also called 'fixed income'.

What is Cash?

Cash includes assets that can be used as money.

It is useful to keep some cash in case you need it for something urgent.

How Cash Investing Works:

The Bank of England sets the official interest rate. (It's called the 'official bank rate'.)

High street banks offer interest-bearing accounts (such as savings accounts), which pay interest on the money that you deposit.

You open an interest-bearing account at a bank.

You deposit money into your account, and it earns interest. That's your return!

There is hardly any risk of losing your capital. You can use it for other things if you want to.

Investing in cash is VERY LOW RISK
It also offers low returns.

What is Property?

Property includes buildings and land.

How Property Investing Works:

You buy a building or a plot of land.

You might choose to invest more capital in the property – like renovating a building or developing land into a neighbourhood with new homes.

After a period of time, you sell the property, hopefully for more than you paid for it.
That's your return!

Or you rent the property out to a tenant.
The rent is your return!

Property is very expensive, and many investors can't afford to invest in it.

Plus, investing in property comes with risks.

What Are Commodities?

Commodities are natural resources & raw materials.

Energy (oil)

Precious Metals

Agricultural Products

Livestock

How Commodity Investing Works:

You can invest directly in commodities.

(For example, you can buy a piece of gold.)

You buy a commodity at its current market value. Then, if its value goes up, you can sell it for more than you paid for it.

That's your return!

But if its value goes down, then you will lose your capital. Boo!

Some investors invest in futures, which are traded on an exchange.

Investing in commodities or futures can be expensive, complicated and risky!

That's How Investing and Asset Management Works!

And we hope this book has answered all of your questions.

"Indeed it has, thanks!"

Asset Management Words

Allocate
to decide how capital is invested

Asset
something that has value, which can be sold or used as money

Asset Class(es)
different types of investments, which each work in their own way

Bank of England
the central bank of the United Kingdom, which looks after our Economy and sets the official interest rate

Benchmark
a tool to measure a fund's performance, usually by comparing it to a specific asset market

Bond
an asset where you let the issuer use your money for a period of time; some people call this asset class 'fixed income'

Broker
a person, company, website or app that buys or sells assets for an investor

Capital
the money used to make an investment

Capital Gains Tax
tax that you may have to pay on your investment returns

Cash
an asset that can be used as money

Commodities
raw materials, such as gold, coffee and energy, that have value

Debt
when you owe someone money

Default
to not repay a debt

Demand
how badly people want something and how much they are willing to pay for it

Diversify
when you protect against risk by putting capital into lots of different investments

Divest
when you sell or get rid of an investment

Dividend
a tiny bit of a company's profit, which is given to investors

Equities
an asset class where investors own a tiny bit of a big, big company

Exchanges
special markets where commodity futures are traded

Factors
causes or reasons

Fee
amount of money that you pay to the person or company who helps you buy or sell an asset

Financial Markets
markets where investment products and assets are bought and sold

Fixed Income
asset class that includes bonds; bond investors receive a fixed income in the form of regular interest payments

Fund(s)
a sum of capital that is used for a specific purpose

Futures
contracts to buy or sell a commodity at a certain price, on a specific future date

Income
money that you receive regularly

Invest
to put money into something in the hope that it will make more money

Investment(s)
the 'something' that you put your money into, hoping for a good return

Investor
the person or institution that makes an investment

Interest
for borrowers, it is the amount of money, on top of the loan amount, that is repaid;

for savers, it is the amount of money added to an interest-bearing account

Interest-Bearing Account(s)
a savings or cash account that allows you to deposit money and earn interest on it

Issuer
the institution that offers bonds or equity shares to investors

Loan
money that is borrowed, usually to be repaid with interest

Market Value
the actual price that a share is bought or sold

Maturity
when a bond has reached the end of its term; this is when investors get their capital back

Negative Return
when the value of your investment goes down and you lose some (or all) of your investment capital

Performance
the value of an investment over a period of time

Portfolio
a collection of investments

Positive Return
when the value of your investment goes up and you get back your investment capital, plus extra money

Priorities
the things that are important to you

Property
something that you own, such as land or a building

Regulations
rules or laws

Return
the 'more money' that you hope to get back when you make an investment

Risk(s)
possibility that something bad might happen

Risk Tolerance
how much risk you are willing to accept in your portfolio

Sector(s)
an industry or area of work

Share
a tiny bit of ownership of a big, big company

Stake
when you invest in something and your capital is part of it

Term
a period of time

Time Horizon
the amount of time that you have before you need a return on your investments

Trader(s)
the people or companies who are allowed to buy and sell in markets

Undervalued
an asset that a fund manager hopes will go up in value

Value
how much something is worth

About the Project

How the World ^{Really} Works **Asset Management** was developed in a collaboration among Schroders employees, students from Moreland Primary School and the Guy Fox team.

Illustrators from Moreland Primary School:
Zion, Cerise, Khadijah, Scarlet, Adam, Tavante, Dahlia, Harvey, Mufed, Anaya, Joel, Dania, Manaar, Israa, Aweis, Tayah, Hajer, Huda, Malachi, Shada, Anderson, Devran, Maryam, Oliver, Sarah, Zhanae and Tyreese-James **Participants:** Shadiyah and Fawaz

Moreland Primary School Staff: Valerie Amissah, Danielle Hammond, Chris Quinton, Karen Hough, Harima Rahim and Beverley Turner

Our Schroders Team: Alex James, Caroline Shaw, Florina Brahimi, Valerie de Jong, Duncan Squire, Hannah Simons, William Andrew, Andy Pearce, Claire Herbert, Emilie Fan, Penny Avraam, Yu Shi Lam, Ben Popatlal, Claire Glennon, Douglas Smith, Jamie Gossage, Claudia Roden, Henrietta McDonald, Julian Hammerton, Laura Whelan, Simon Winchcombe, Francesca Guinane, Pippa O'Riley, Vanessa Lazarski, Lana Kamffer, Meriel Crawford, Nicole Howard, Alex Bellamy, Orvin Davidson, Cheryl Hiew, Sophie Whitwell, Fatna Chelihi, Andrew Lacey, Elizabeth Conmy, Peter Harrison and Louisa Minter-Kemp

With Thanks to: Laura Davies, Jo Westhead, Colin McDonald and Kate Douglas

Guy Fox Staff & Volunteers: Piera Lizzeri, Sam Moore, Marie Schädel, Kate Clark, Simon J. Harper, Fiona Galvin Rhymer, Kaisa Patsalides, Breda Keating and Kourtney Harper